Beauregard Houston-Montgomery

Here, a 1940s lithographed tin dollhouse (by Meritoy of Boston, Mass.) neatly represents the original time period in which *Peyton Place* was set. The staircase seen through the window is from a sprawling 1950s Louis Marx & Co. dollhouse. For whatever reasons, very few of these metal, or earlier fiberboard, dollhouses had even lithographed stairways.

Endpapers from Amloid Company's My Dolly's House packaging.

DOLLHOUSE LIVING

fotofolio

THE DOLLHOUSE: MICROCOSM OF THE LIFE DREAM

We begin building our own worlds with the sticks and stones of our childhood. These dream worlds manifest how we process our fears and longings, the things beyond our control during the tender, intense years when we are little people.

When Beauregard was growing up, beauty was not easy to access. Retreating into the mini-worlds of dollhouses went against his gender. Yet he intuitively sought out these models of fantasy and order, subliminally understanding they led to inhabiting the bigger picture. His fascination did not diminish with years.

Beauregard's journey from a young child finding the perfect escape to a serious, committed, and completely obsessive collector is both moving and astonishing, as the reader realizes that the misery children go through when they are denied their passions can become their greatest strength.

Beauregard brought stability to his migratory and precarious youth by claiming his right to explore and collect dolls and dollhouses. When disaster struck and all his dolls and dollhouses were "lost" by the moving van when he was 10, he resorted to the pages of the Sears Christmas Toy catalog to rebuild his fantasies.

As kids we all have our version of the safe house—that place we establish or concoct where it's ok to be ourselves, or where we have much more fun being our better selves. For me, growing up in Manhattan, Betty and Veronica's suburban lifestyle in the pages of *Archie* comic books was it. Beauregard became mesmerized by the artifacts of style around him no matter where he ended up. Whether it was an attic full of vintage toys, or catalogs detailing the range of housing possibilities, or a cluster of deserted cabins in the woods, he sensed that the elements of style could be edited and personalized to reinvent the world.

Timothy Greenfield-Sanders first mentioned Beauregard's apartment to me, knowing my penchant for unusual living spaces. My editorial curiosity became raging fascination once I understood he wasn't describing a mere collector's lair, but rather a tiny railroad apartment completely taken over by force of fantasy. Every surface, every single inch of Beauregard's apartment, is filled to the ceiling with his meticulously ordered collection. It is a veritable museum of the history of the genre, a wonder world in miniature in a miniature apartment. The only clearing is Beauregard's double bed, and it is here that he records his magical settings with a simple camera and handheld flashlight. These extraordinary photographs bring Beauregard's passion and his determination to mine his dreams full circle.

ATOMIC TRAILER PARK

As a child in the 1950s, my parents moved a lot, leaving me with a profound, if superficial, longing for gorgeous geographic and domestic consistency. Before I was three, my father, a Marine

recruiter, transferred us from the lusciously tropical terrain of Honolulu, to Arts-and-Craftsy San Diego, and then to a Cape Cod cottage by scenic Crystal Lake, New Hampshire. I had an anxiety

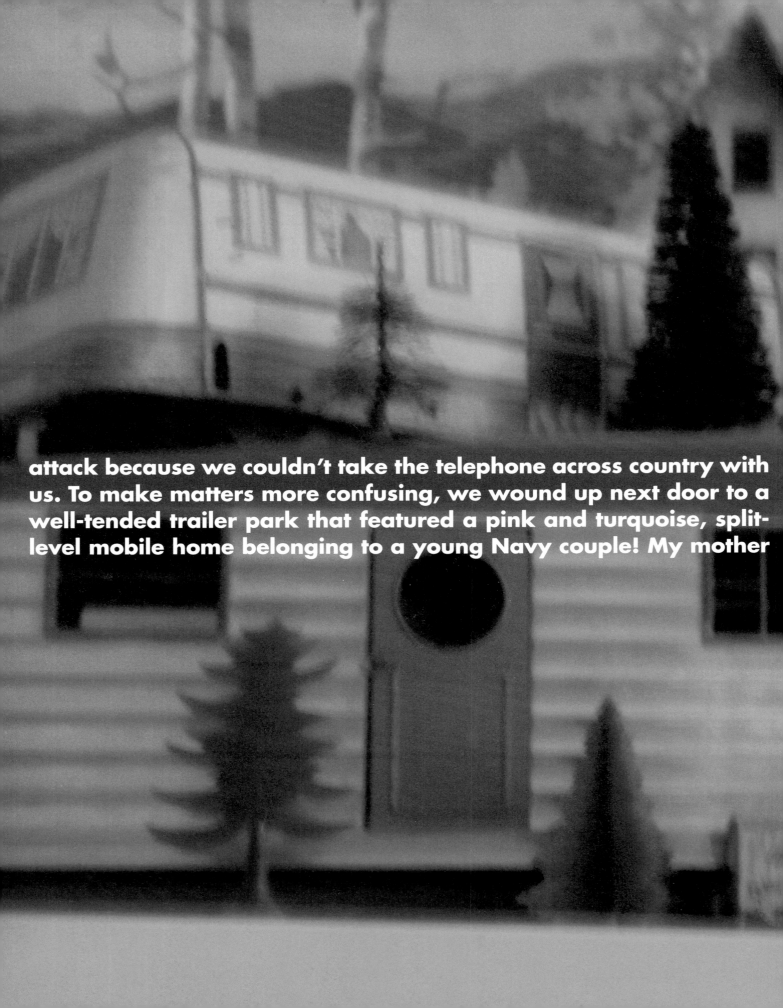

attack because we couldn't take the telephone across country with us. To make matters more confusing, we wound up next door to a well-tended trailer park that featured a pink and turquoise, split-level mobile home belonging to a young Navy couple! My mother

was appalled that I preferred their brightly colored, metal butter-fly chairs and the all-out atomic ambience of the exotic tin can next door to our own dull *I Love Lucy* eclectic furnishings, which seemed silly set in the pragmatic context of the little cottage.

Portrayed in advertisements at the back of shelter magazines as smart leisure homes, the reality of the trailers would only be perceived long after my visual references had been idealized.

Plasticville U.S.A., Bachmann, Ohio Art, Nylint, and kitchmeister Franklin Mint are all represented in these tiny trailers created from the 1930s to the 1990s.

PEYTON PLACES

While I dutifully tried to repress my atomic-modern yearnings, my less than idyllic early youth was marked by being stalked by a serial child-killer, attacked by a pack of wild dogs, and drowning in Crystal Lake. Little did I realize that nearby a book was taking shape that would realistically reflect the rapid changes middle-class America was undergoing. Behind the cheerful chintz curtains and pristinely painted clapboard of picture-postcard perfect *Peyton Place*, seethed social conflicts that would soon sweep the consciousness of American popular culture.

My own introduction to this literary page-turner came from its creator, Grace Metalious, who on occasion played pinochle (or was it poker?) at the atomic trailer. While, in retrospect, I have the highest regard for the self-doomed, somewhat epicene author, mini-me was as judgmental as the tightly knit town of Gilmanton, on which *Peyton Place* is based. Unlike the town's "kill the messenger" mentality, my own disapproval was rooted in Grace's greasy hair and perennial cloud of cigarette smoke. My chief amusement at these otherwise (for me, anyway) boring parties was the Felix the Cat clock in the kitchen corridor, which would roll its eyes at me with metronomic regularity, lamenting, I assumed, the endless tedium of allegedly adult human behavior.

It was the lavishly lensed, 20th Century Fox Cinemascope version of *Peyton Place*, released in 1957, that would influence my dollhouse consciousness, beautifully realizing my earliest imaginings of what the world should look like. Just as I longed to see the film version of *Peyton Place* over and over to memorize it visually, so I desperately desired dollhouses to act out my fantasies and idealizations. Having always felt like a space alien, I found refuge in the familiarity of the classic Cape Cod in which my idol Allison grew up. It is the quintessential American home, as versatile as it

As portrayed by the delicious Mary Astor in *Return to Peyton Place*, Roberta Carter dwelled in a gloomy, sheet-shrouded mini-manse that was both back lot and union in decor. Here I pay homage with my own version of one of Mary Astor's last sets. The dollhouse is late 1940s lithographed tin from Playsteel, for the American Can Corporation. The furniture is from a variety of 1950s toy companies, including Louis Marx & Co.

Early one Christmas, I awoke to a wealth of unwanted toy trains and trucks, and howled until my father went into Manchester to the little toy store, and knocked on the proprietor's door. He opened up his shop downstairs, and sold my red-faced parent the pink-haired Schiaparelli doll I had demanded with such conviction, previously in vain.

FRIENDLY FOLKS
MOTEL

VACANCY

★ LUXURY-REST
  MATTRESS

★ AUTRONIC
  TELEVISION

★ PURE-AIR
  CONDITIONING

★ WARM-AIR
  RADIANT HEAT

★ LUX-O
  TOWELS

★ SNUG-FIT
  CONTOUR SHEETS

★ VENIZIAN FLOOR
  COVERINGS

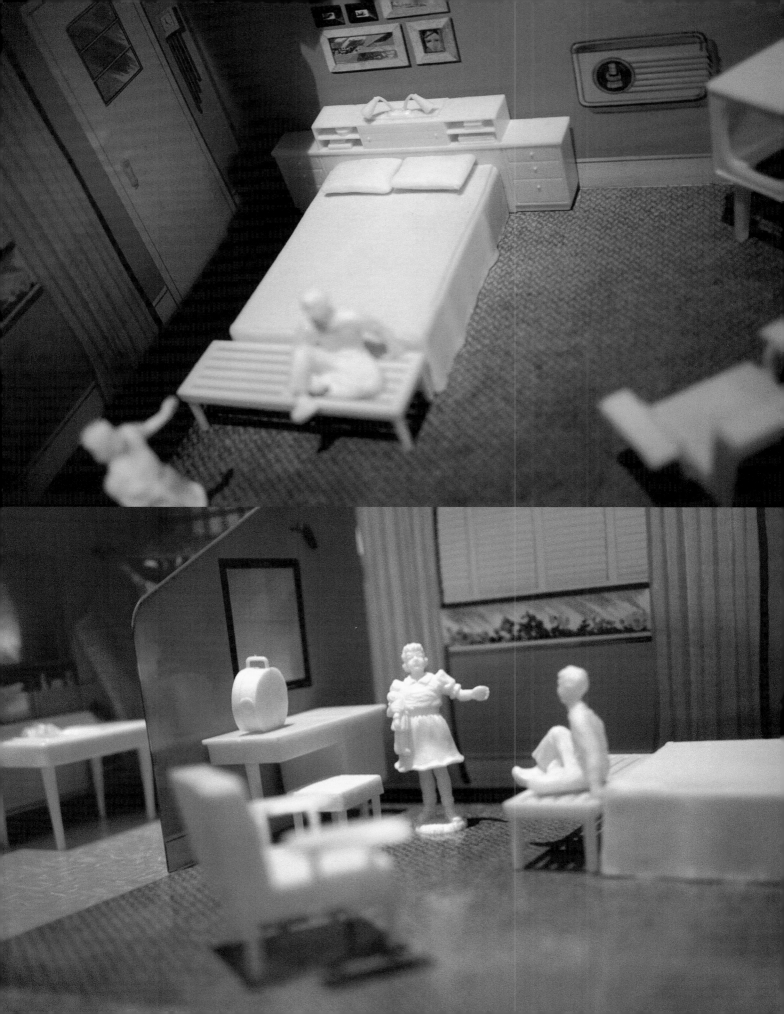

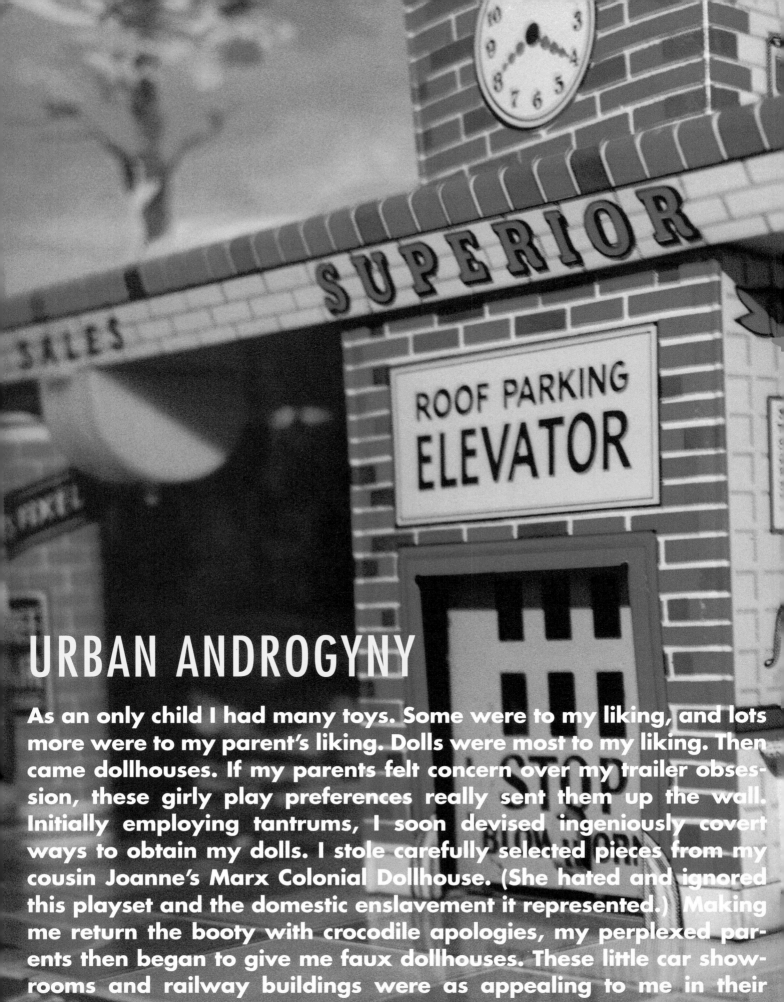

URBAN ANDROGYNY

As an only child I had many toys. Some were to my liking, and lots more were to my parent's liking. Dolls were most to my liking. Then came dollhouses. If my parents felt concern over my trailer obsession, these girly play preferences really sent them up the wall. Initially employing tantrums, I soon devised ingeniously covert ways to obtain my dolls. I stole carefully selected pieces from my cousin Joanne's Marx Colonial Dollhouse. (She hated and ignored this playset and the domestic enslavement it represented.) Making me return the booty with crocodile apologies, my perplexed parents then began to give me faux dollhouses. These little car show-rooms and railway buildings were as appealing to me in their

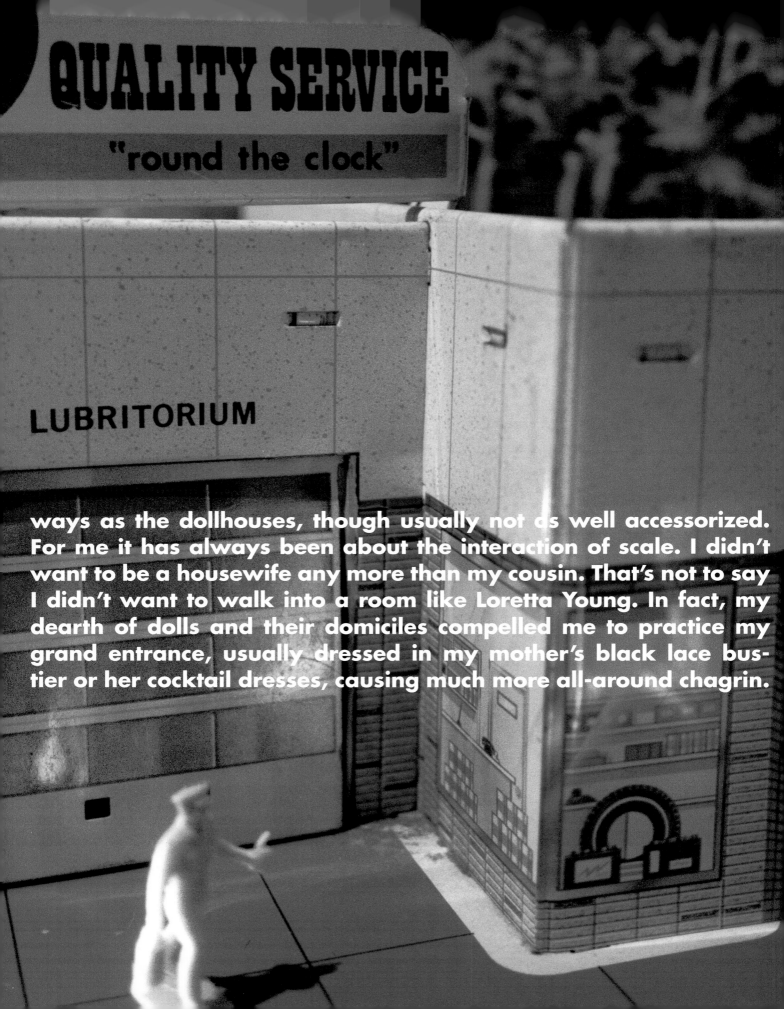

QUALITY SERVICE

"round the clock"

LUBRITORIUM

ways as the dollhouses, though usually not as well accessorized. For me it has always been about the interaction of scale. I didn't want to be a housewife any more than my cousin. That's not to say I didn't want to walk into a room like Loretta Young. In fact, my dearth of dolls and their domiciles compelled me to practice my grand entrance, usually dressed in my mother's black lace bustier or her cocktail dresses, causing much more all-around chagrin.

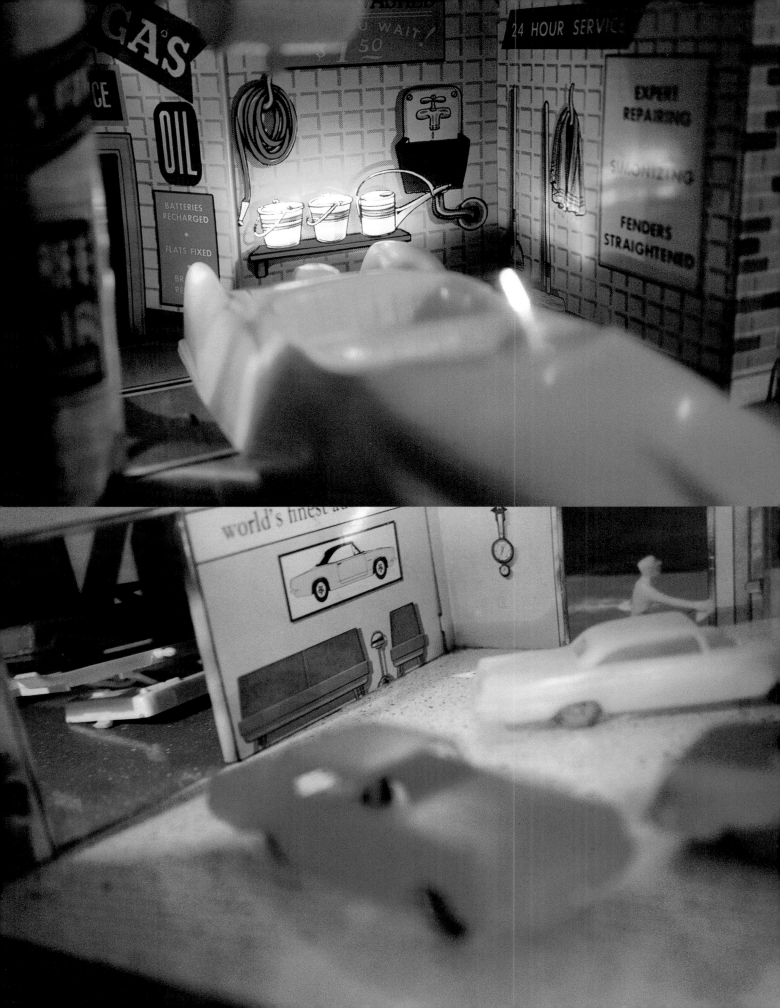

Louis Marx & Co.'s rare Skyscraper playset was produced briefly in the early 1950s. Neither a dollhouse nor a filling station, it was too androgynous for parents anxious to instill proper gender identity in baby boomers.

ICONIC TARA

At age six, the year *Peyton Place* was first published, we moved far away to the midwest, to a tiny Missouri town near my maternal grandparent's picturesque farm. Their white clapboard Gothic gabled farmhouse with the tin roof had been constructed around the turn of the century. Built on a rise that surveyed the countryside for miles, Hilltop Farm was surrounded by whitewashed wooden fences enclosing fields of grazing cattle which would, with regularity, turn up curiously mutilated. With its pristine red barn, red and white outbuildings, poplars and Japanese pine trees, and grassy-mound tornado shelter, this place was a Bruce Weber location come to life.

With my father away in Asia, my mother and I lived on the top floor of a large Arts-and-Crafts style house in the nearby town, which was built around a square. Little had changed since the early part of the century. As was the custom in the little enclave,

the house in which we lived had been built from plans found in a catalog. Indeed, catalogs supplied much of the merchandise, there being no malls. They also supplied dolls and the popular lithographed metal dollhouses, including the farm playset my parents cursed at assembling one Christmas eve.

I pored over and memorized these catalogs with far more enthusiasm than I had for learning how to read. Forsaking all hope of absorbing anything but alienation at school, I found my grandmother's first edition of *Gone With The Wind* and taught myself how to read by age seven. It was easy to imagine the white-columned porch of the farmhouse possessing the greater allure of Tara. I sat upstairs in the unfinished "junkroom" and soaked up Scarlett and Melanie, knowing full well that I was the former and would surely go straight to hell.

Reclining amidst my mother's and her sisters' old toys, I studied vintage catalogs from the 1930s and 1940s that were stacked in the corner, along with dozens of dress patterns dating back to the teens and 20s. There was a filigree toaster, and a telephone from the era of the Titanic, along with a lurid book written at the time of its sinking. This was my grandmother's style archives, and I devoured it all summer.

The terrain and woods nearby were peppered with little, decaying cabins that had been built by the original settlers, and these pre-suburban artifacts also fascinated me. They were celebrated in a variety of novelty homages that had been reproduced and sold since the turn of the century. My favorite was one my pizazzy Aunt Helen (who had a fondness for the color blue, particularly in mir-rored furniture) had on her sun porch. It was an elaborate cabin made of grapevines, fancifully transformed into a table which held pipes and tobacco. I never forgot it.

I also never forgot Tara. I memorized the film version, even draw-
ing up floor plans of its layout. It would be six years before
the re-release of the Selznick Civil War propaganda epic, and
it was the pressed-board pillared dollhouses in the 1930s and
1940s catalogs (usually manufactured by Rich Toy Co.) that
originally fueled my vision of this iconic, glorified farmhouse.

CURATORIALLY CORRECT

My thirst for a gorgeous geographic and social context was quenched when, at age seven, my parents moved us to Williamsburg, Virginia. Best described as a colonial theme park, it was less Disney and more in the manner of the then tender-aged Martha Stewart. Within the "restricted" area, only three buildings were inconsistent with the Rockefeller restoration. One was the awesomely Gothic à la Hammer Film insane asylum, since torn down. The other two were Colonial houses that had been remodeled in Victorian times. These shabby but chic enclaves were owned by old school, already ancient siblings, who held out

against the town's reigning restoration mentality. (When the sisters in one house recently expired, their proud, dignified domain was set upon almost immediately by archaeologists.)

Somehow having convinced my parents to take me to see the visually breathtaking film version of *Peyton Place*, the back lot perfection of Williamsburg seemed a scenic combination of North and South: pristinely restored salt boxes set amidst dense forests showed tangible touches of Tara. Best of all was the world's largest boxwood maze, although its glory has since faded.

HOW DEFT IS DELMER DAVES

While I was solidifying the subtleties of North and South, another consciousness was bombarding me at the movies – that of an American auteur named Delmer Daves. In Daves' highly entertaining and precise *A Summer Place*, the implacable actress Dorothy

Maguire (in a manner that would make Nancy Reagan pea green with envy) says to pathos-soaked superstar Sandra Dee, "Frank Lloyd Wright designed our house...," as she leads her into an astounding abode built into a Pacific coast cliff, passing as Maine.

The subtext of this film seemed to be that as the cheating parents progressed beyond motels, they moved from stately, separate, (and drafty) colonial abodes to one chic ultra-modern palace in an even more desirable neighborhood. *Peyton Place*'s changing mores were dramatically reflected in the decor of its inhabitants.

This modern Meritous fashion doll pavilion is a paean to the deco decor of Miami's trendy South Beach. Here it serves as a high-tech tribute to Delmer Daves' decor, or perhaps the *Tab Hunter Show*'s Malibu House.

With their *Summer Place* symbiosis, these 1980s and 1990s plastic Meritous dollhouses could easily be set in the affluent environs of Long Island's Hamptons, an exasperating enclave that combines the provincial air of *Peyton Place*, the colonial context of Williamsburg, and the show biz decadence of *Valley of the Dolls*.

Reminiscent of the California ski resort sub-text in the movie *Return to Peyton Place,* this unmarked, A-frame house (probably 1970s Fisher-Price) is filled with 1990s fairy furniture from Kennar.

Just as decor was changing in movies and television, so the lithographed metal dollhouses of Louis Marx & Co. (though for the most part physically unchanged) underwent graphic transformations that replaced knotty pine and chintz with Chinese Modern.

LE PETIT CHATEAU DE BRIGITTE BARDOT

When I was six and still in the little Missouri town, every Saturday I would go unattended to the small movie theater (which later was used for years to hold secret militia meetings, and eventually burned) for a second-run matinee. It was here I soaked up the astounding, subversively androgynous film *Funny Face*, which primed me for the fashion doll that was about to revolutionize the world of dolls and their houses. I also saw a hypnotic movie called *Bonjour Tristesse*, which had fashions so memorable that, although I didn't see the film again for 30 years, I remembered every outfit. Equally memorable was the Riviera vacation villa inhabited by a dazzlingly nubile Jean Seberg, who portrayed an haute couture version of Allison MacKenzie, living *la dolce vita*. (Audrey Hepburn's *Funny Face*, on the other hand, was a beatnik Allison.)

In the 1990s my friend Allison (not exactly MacKenzie) gave me a dollhouse reminiscent of this Riviera house. From the Swedish company Lundby, this spacious doll villa seemed the perfect place to display my 1960s Ideal Petite Princess doll furniture. It was this short-lived line (marketed as both Petite Princess and Princess Patti) that influenced later doll furnishing designs to become more detailed, if not more fanciful.

The most decadent of mass-manufactured, 20th century American toy furniture, Petite Princess was anathema to parents (not just mine) who were appalled at the blatant Hollywood vulgarity. Detailed workmanship meant high prices, and just as parents shunned the line, their children obsessed on it. As a result, the once forbidden pieces can still be found in their original boxes at undiminished prices by grown children seeking long deferred gratification.

These glamorous fantasy furnishings were a dramatic departure from the traditional, poured-plastic examples that had filled dollhouses previously. This was the kind of furniture with which Eva Gabor would fill Green Acres. Petite Princess furniture exuded the campy *Cleopatra* consciousness that anticipated the excesses of the impending psychedelic explosion.

While arranging the pieces in the house to photograph for this book, I read an item on "Page Six" in the *New York Post* about actress Catherine Deneuve, criticizing French legend Brigitte Bardot. It seems Mme. Deneuve called Mme. Bardot "hopeless" because she long ago gave up on her own allure, and now wastes her time saving animals. As I icily placed the Petite Princess pieces, the house was no longer the deadly playground of Ms. Seberg's narcissistic character Cecile. Instead, it evolved into la Bardot's villa, filled with her dogs waiting for their mistress to come back from lunch with another patron saint of animals, the divine Doris Day.

LILLIPUTIAN LEVITTOWN

When I was 10 years old two hideous things happened. First, my balls dropped. While I eventually reconciled myself to that nightmare, the family move to a small, generic midwestern city looms to this day as a horror in my fragile mind. Not far from the once cinematic little village near my grandparents' home (which was being torn down, paved over, and vinyl-sided), this population-100,000 armpit of a town had a fertilizer plant downtown, as

well as 15 Bible colleges, and Jerry Falwell's (or was it Jimmie Swaggart's?) world headquarters. Needless to say, moving from a curatorially correct Martha Stewart environment to this dismal province where everything was brown, preferably polyester, and everyone seemed slow and mean-spirited, did not sit well with the onslaught of my adolescence.

The dismal isolation of my time in suburbia, illustrated on the preceding page b
Amloid Company's *My Dolly's House*, wa
assuaged by the reassuring, mostly Marx
lithographed tin ranch and split-level dol
houses which follow.

Upon arrival I was told all my carefully collected and much coveted dolls and miniatures had been "lost" in the moving van. I had only the Sears Christmas Toy catalog on which to project my idealistic fantasies of how to adapt to this dreary locale. The catalog dollhouses of the day were styled after the contemporary ranch-homes that had taken over the supposedly safe, and definitely stifling, suburbs in which we (and everyone else, it seemed) now

lived. I lavished a great deal of attention on the television version of *Peyton Place*, an ongoing soap opera starring Mia Farrow as Allison, perfectly cast to update my heroine into the thoroughly modern 1960s. I replicated the drawings used at the beginning of the television show to depict Fox's *Peyton Place*, no longer the 1950s cinema rendition. My dollhouse *Peyton Place*, by geographic necessity, had turned into a 1960s Lilliputian Levittown.

Our own Williamsburg-style ranch house, so reassuringly generic in every way, could have been one of these dollhouses. I spent hours on end transforming the house while my anxious parents were at their jobs. After being ridiculed as a "freak of

Two of my most passionate goals as a teenager in the 1960s were to replace my father's E-Z Boy recliner with an Eames lounge chair, and to incorporate an Azuma hanging-basket chair into our Manson family room. By the 1980s I had done both.

nature" in biology class by a teacher, who took issue with my fey demeanor, I went to school as little as possible as an act of self-preservation, wary of my ability to withstand the ongoing assault on my self-esteem.

I survived the depression brought on from living in Podunk by subscribing to Diana Vreeland's *Vogue*, obsessing on the movie *Cleopatra*, and saving my erupting skin by arranging an appoint-

In the 1970s, dollhouses like this Tomy Smaller Homes and Gardens evolved from the previous traditional examples to a more detailed Contemporary Modern, reflecting the looser *Brady Bunch* lifestyle Americans were living.

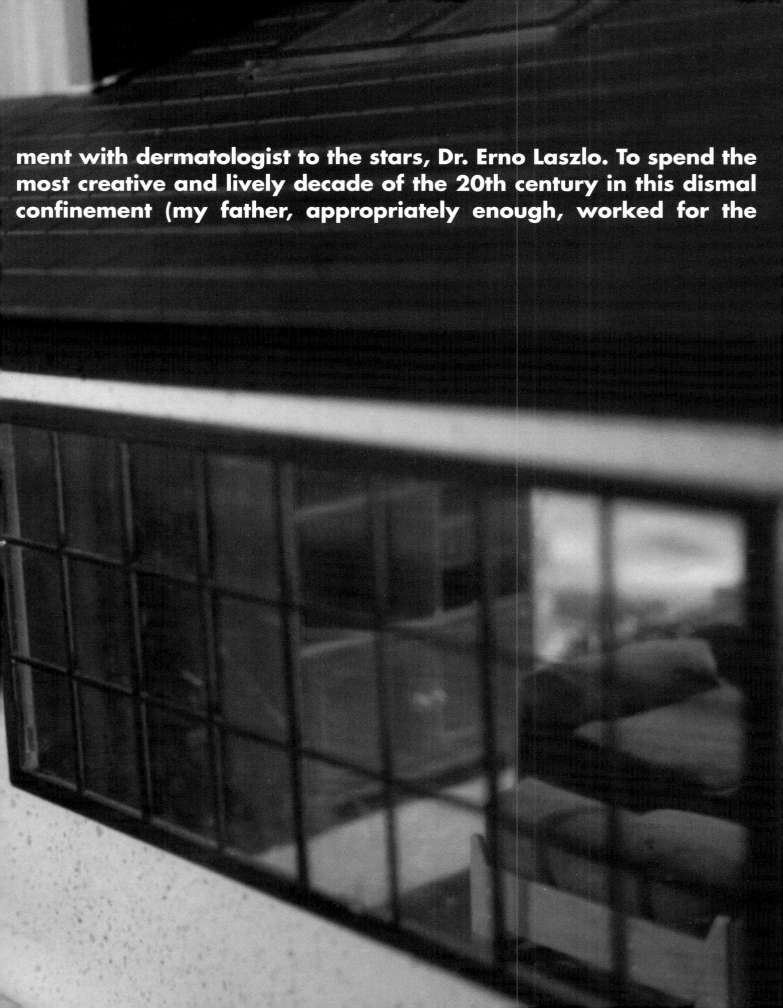

ment with dermatologist to the stars, Dr. Erno Laszlo. To spend the most creative and lively decade of the 20th century in this dismal confinement (my father, appropriately enough, worked for the

Federal Bureau of Prisons) was a nightmare, so I did the only thing I could. I knew, like Allison, what I wanted from life: to go to the city, become completely sophisticated, and simply rise above

it all. I devoted myself to studying for imminent escape and its potential consequences. My textbook was the phenomenal successor to *Peyton Place*, Jacqueline Susann's *Valley of the Dolls*.

WAY BEYOND THE VALLEY OF THE DOLLS

Valley of the Dolls is the real sequel to *Peyton Place*. Androgynous Allison becomes the drop-dead gorgeous Anne Wells, and *Peyton Place* turns into Lawrenceville. (In the movie version it was really glamorous and cushy Bedford, N.Y., just as Peyton Place was really sumptuously scenic Camden, Maine.) Like Allison and myself, "Dolls" heroine Anne Wells had no taste for farm living with its turgid fecundity. She went to Manhattan looking for adventure and sophistication (and in the subtext of Barbara Parkins' film performance as Anne, distraction from

some unnamed panic: Did she too feel like a space alien?). Anne's story, along with that of her pals Neely and Jennifer, could be a textbook on modern celebrity life. All that's missing are the cell phones. So aptly named, the film version of *Valley of the Dolls* could also serve as a textbook on fashion doll living. Barbie®, the most notable fashion doll, burst upon the toy world in 1959. Like nothing before or since, parents hated this doll just as much as children (of both sexes, and for a variety of reasons) wanted her.

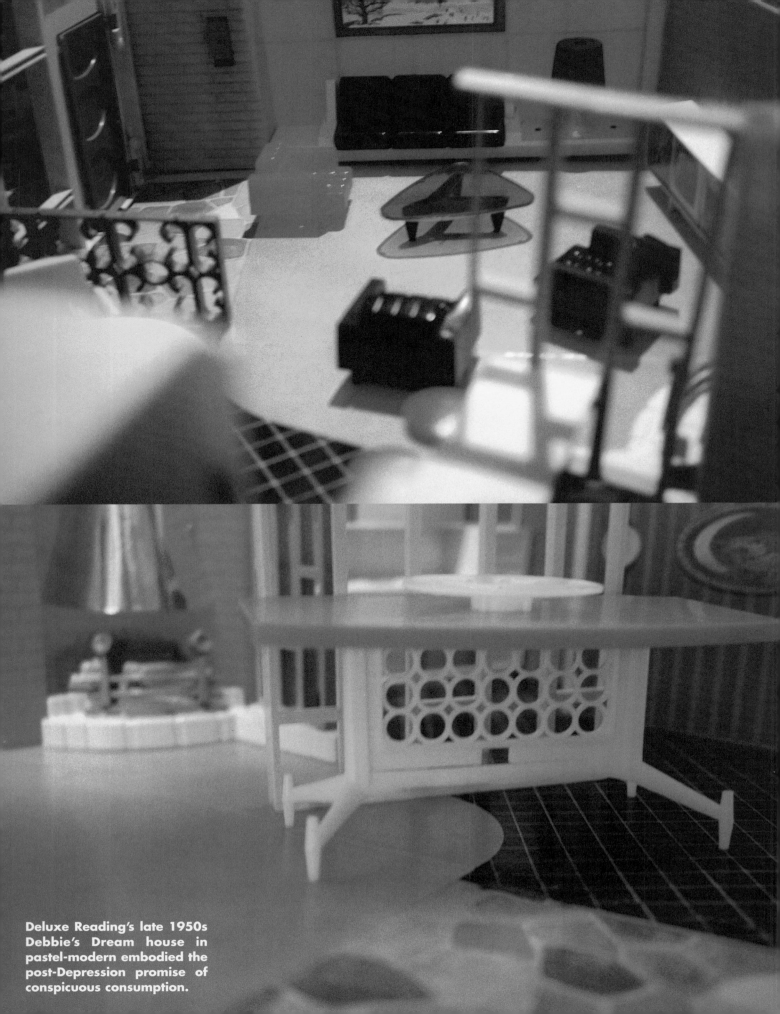

Deluxe Reading's late 1950s Debbie's Dream house in pastel-modern embodied the post-Depression promise of conspicuous consumption.

Naturally, the children won out. The first children's doll represented as an adult (previously, even fashion dolls had the mien of little Jon Benet Ramsey-type mannequins), the 11 1/2-inch Barbie® doll was originally morphed from the German Bild Lily doll, which was based on a slutty adult comic strip character. She was redone in the image of the Barbie® doll's ingenious fashion designer, Charlotte Johnson, a sophisticated woman of the world. Although Barbie® and her clones seemed to me more akin to a dominatrix-demeanored Joan Crawford than any teenager, their lifestyles were so chicly art directed they were irresistible.

Unlike dollhouse dolls, who were mere accessories to their houses, fashion dolls lived in a brave new world that revolved around them. The traditional dollhouses that had ruled since the 1950s seemed obsolete compared to the oversized (though never quite fashion-doll scale) folding cardboard cases and plastic containers that housed the glittering fashion doll universe. Their sleekly contemporary and elaborate Louis furnishings and accoutrements flaunted a fashionable world of glamorous consumerism. By the end of the 1960s, fashion dolls had gone completely Mod. Now considered not only the wrong sex, but too old to play with them, I persisted in going to the fashion-doll section the Sears Catalog first.

Miss Seventeen (who looked like she was going on forty), Marx's 15-inch version of Bild Lily, relaxes in a 1970s catalog-issue swimming pool playset.

Presumably well-intentioned "experts" suggested I try "altering my gender" as a way to acceptably play with dolls (and eventually men). Beyond anorexia, thank heavens I never had a penchant for self-mutilation!

In 1969, Topper Toys came up with a doll who could have walked out of the pages of *Valley of the Dolls*. Her name was Dawn, and she was half the size of the Barbie® doll, with a lot more style. According to her designer, Nick Grandee, her delightful allure was modeled on a Holly Golightly-type named Susan who was greatly admired at the soon-to-expire toy company. By now, however, I had moved to Manhattan and was thriving so I didn't give Dawn or the other fashion dolls much thought. I was too busy living their fantasy lifestyles. Although my self-esteem had been obliterated by the schools I was forced to attend, I made up for it in attitude, and was living *la dolce vita* with a vengeance. If, to quote Quentin Crisp, Joan Crawford could be radioactive with self-belief, so could I. By the end of the 1970s, I was doing my graduate work in sociology at Studio 54 and was as blasé as Jean Seberg in *Bonjour Tristesse*.

Dollhouse dolls, previously staid little mannequins from such companies as Flagg Doll Co., got a fashion doll makeover with Kennar's 1981, 4-inch Glamour Gals, an agency of fashion models who hung out with handsome boyfriends in this Glamour Gals' Party Place.

During the 1980s I found myself writing for fashionable magazines with entrée into some of the world's most exclusive, not to mention rarefied and esoteric, enclaves. In 1984, however, I would re-enter the fashion doll universe because of my friend Andy Warhol, whom I met at a Barbie® party at the Waldorf Astoria, where he went out of his way to charm me (not that it was very difficult) into working for his magazine, *Interview*. He took pics of me, along with all his "celebutant" workers, one of which wound up in *Andy Warhol's Party Book*. It didn't matter that drinking was ruining my life, but the fact that I appeared in a two-page spread looking like Sally Jessy Raphael made me give up alcohol immediately. Compelled to quench my thirst elsewhere, I took another cue from Andy and started shopping compulsively. Tapping into my repressed longing for dolls and dollhouses, Kiddie City and Toys 'R' Us became familiar haunts, as did flea markets.

Had *Valley of the Dolls'* Anne, Neely, and Jennifer survived into the 1970s, they might have wound up on *Charlie's Angels*, performing in this elevated, revolving Charlie's Angels Hide-Away House from Hasbro. The inevitably pink Eames-style chair and ottoman is a modern Barbie® piece.

By the 1990s I was no longer fashion-able. Hair had stopped growing on my head and started growing in my nose. My forehead broke out in wrinkles and acne, and there was no longer a Dr. Laszlo to run to. I stopped living *la dolce vita* and turned into Juliet of the Spirits. Depression, like some inevitable relative, made a return visit.

Although I realize homosexuals are not legally allowed to marry, like Anne Wells in *Valley of the Dolls*, I had a faithless husband during much of my return to doll and dollhouse collecting. He would have preferred I drink to my being an embarrassing old Barbie® queen and whined that I should focus on something that interested him, like antique English china. I continued to buy my toys surreptitiously, knowing that this might be the only real estate I'd ever be able to obtain. I stashed most of the treasures I bought in storage to shut him up.

The 1980s Transformers trend influenced this tiny Boutique from Arrow Ind., Inc., which transforms from a tightly contained cube into a veritable strip mall.

After 12 years, the time came to pack hubby's things. I sent them to storage and brought all my toys to my apartment. (A valuable lesson from Jackie Onassis: Never give up your own apartment!) As I sat forlorn, delusions dissolved, completely surrounded by dozens of dusty containers of toys, dolls, and dollhouses, I realized that this was my midlife crisis. It could have been so much worse.

Tuesday Taylor's Ideal 1970s life style included this plush, modular Manhattan penthouse-cum-artist's studio, along with a hunky blond boyfriend, Eric. The heart chair is from Vitra Design Museum Miniature collection.

THE HOUSE OF THE FUTURE

Since the mid-20th century, dollhouses have featured electric lights and doorbells. By the 1980s, electronic sounds were added to enhance play value. Today's world is being transformed by the internet, making even the miracle of television seem outmoded. It will be fascinating to see how dollhouses' limited space will be expanded by the increasingly tiny components that are revolutionizing the unlimited realm of cyberspace. Although gifted with such limited precognition that I can't seem to forecast beyond lunch most days, I can predict I'll be perusing the aisles of F.A.O. Schwarz, checking out the latest little real estate, for the rest of my life in the 21st century.

Contemporary modern is usually as close as "dollhouses of the future" get to forward forecasts. In the 1970s, however, Kennar's Bionic Woman Jamie Sommers doll's high tech, inflatable geodesic dome home had Palladian windows that forecast the post-modern movement, just as its electronic theme (depicted only with graphics) predicted the eventual computerization of the world.

Author/photographer Beauregard Houston-Montgomery has written for many publications, from *World of Interiors* to *Torso*. His two previous books are *Pouf Pieces* (Hanuman 1990) and *Designer Fashion Dolls* (Hobby House 1999). He currently lives in Manhattan under the protection of rent stabilization laws, which is a blessing, since no trailer park would have him.

© 2000 Beauregard Houston-Montgomery
Fotofolio 561 Broadway, New York, New York 10012
Printed in China
Library of Congress Catalog Card Number: 00-190936
ISBN: 1-58418-023-4

Dedicated to Timothy, Karin, Isca, and Liliana Greenfield-Sanders, and also to my father, Wil Stretch, who eventually bought me all my favorite dollhouses, and my late mother, Jenell McConnell Stretch, who always drew the line at lawn ornaments.

Special Thanks to Martin Bondell and Julie Galant, Benita Cassar Torreggianni, Wendy Goodman, Michael Musto, Mario Buatta, John Darcy Noble, Cindy Adams, Patrick McMullin, Cathy Che, Stephanie Chernikowski, Carolyn Cook, Harry King and Orazio Fortunato, Max Vadukal, Anna and Ciro Musto, Pito Collas, Oliver Rish, Susan Weidenfeld, Kyle Bradford, Alice Hudson, Colleen Moore, Laura Meisner, William Frederick Tropp, Laura Pettibone, Allison Moore, Betty Jane Haden, Colin Shanley, Ruth Handler, Andé Whyland, David Sage, Elizabeth Racine, Sylvia Miles, Zohra Lampert, Pamela Tiffin, Diane Varsi, Mia Farrow, André and Dory Previn, Brigid Berlin, Barbara Parkins, Mariska and Mickey Hargitay, Laurie Campbell, Brian and Sonia Goodfellow, Nick Grandee, Heidi, Natascha and Ruben Bansie/Snellman, Michael Torres and Ryan Lance, John Diamandis, Karen Tina Harrison, Patti Lewis, Yla Eason, Paul Silver, Bradford Samuel, Charles Elkain, Loretta Young, Mr. Kenneth, Ron Schick, Kim Novak, Doris Day, Monica Cohen, Elizabeth Taylor, John deCuir, my dog Frankie, and the late, lamented John Puzewski, Andy Warhol, Grace Metalious, Jacqueline Susann, Jackie Onassis, Franz Waxman, Minnie McConnell, Elmira Montgomery, Bernard Herrmann, Jean Seberg, Audrey Hepburn, Kay Thompson, William Travilla, Peter Hujar, Sidney Guilaroff, Greta Garbo, and Quentin Crisp.

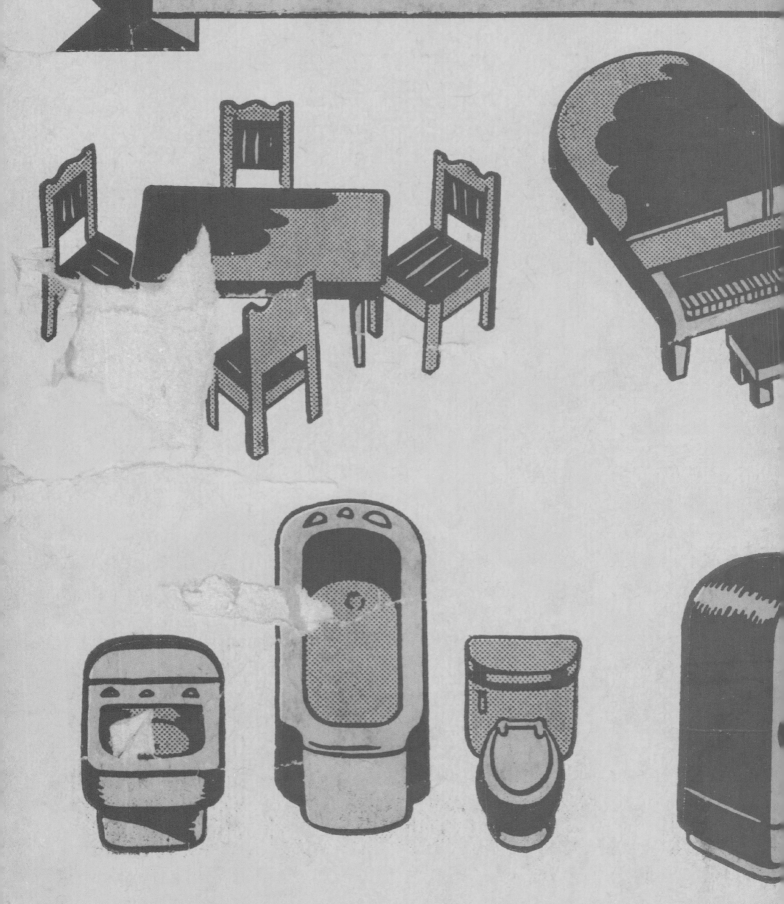